FOOLISH TRUST

*Life in the Unwelcome Tension
between Faith and Reason*

by

RONALD C. GELAUDE

Author of:

The Religion of Jesus

Crazy Shepherd, Crazy Sheep

ISBN: 150854204X

ISBN 13: 9781508542049

Library of Congress Control Number: 2013920590
CreateSpace Independent Publishing Platform
North Charleston, South Carolina

Dedicated To Those:

Who seek *answers from a seemingly silent God*

Who wonder *where he is when you truly need him*

Who wrestle *with the empty space between faith and reason...*

just like me.

In memory of:

Christina Faith Davis,

December 11, 2014–December 17, 2014.

She was a true fighter and a gift beyond my wildest dreams.

Those Who Make It Possible

As in the other books I've written, below is a short list of people who have not only helped make the writing of this book a reality, but who have also made my life both meaningful and rich in more ways than I can describe. Janet Olson Gelaude, together we've realized that God's promises are exceedingly true and his unwavering faithfulness never ends. When I thought it would never happen, you showed up as an unexpected gift. Don and Martha, once again, you've always been there to support and encourage me in my darkest times, and when I wonder if writing and expressing my thoughts and feelings is even worth it. Ken and Pat, together we miss Mike so very much. You've influenced my life more than you'll ever know, and Ken, thanks for your help with the photo artwork on the cover. Bob, Pam, Sandy, Don, Martha, Drew, and Amy, thanks again for proofreading my manuscripts and encouraging me to stay the course.

I also want express my deepest thanks to Fruitland Evangelical Covenant Church in Whitehall, Michigan. Much of this book was written during my time as your Interim Pastor. At a time when I "couldn't wait to run away to places unknown" you entered my life. Over our ten months together you gracefully walked with me side by side, and in doing so, you fostered a setting where I could begin to truly heal. I especially want to thank the Worship Team. Our time together was rich. Thanks for welcoming me into your group.

As you know, playing music has a way of soothing the soul, especially playing the blues with Dan. I'm convinced that it was out of God's tender mercy that he brought us together and I'm extremely grateful for all of you.

As I've mentioned before, these are the dream makers in my life of dreaming what's next. So, what's on the horizon?

Ordinary Virtue | *A True Story and Why It Matters*

Table of Contents

Faith and reason, like two rails of a railroad track,
Seem to merge in the distance of time.
The longer and farther you walk,
They never do.

—Ron (July 28, 2013)

Preface

At my very core, I'm an eternal optimist and remain so, but over the years I've also noticed that life rarely, if ever, works out as planned. At times the pursuit of happiness seems fruitless as we experience setbacks, heartbreak, and disappointment. Simply take notice of our world filled with unexplainable stories of tragedy and loss. Life's not fair. Over the past ten years or so, I've come to the realization that life doesn't always make sense. God doesn't always make sense. Our struggles, more often than we care to admit, leave us with questions for which there seem to be no plausible answers: Why does God do this, but not that? Why does God allow whatever may be happening to happen? During my darkest hours, I've found myself wondering where God was when I needed him most. During these times he never offered me direct answers, and there I sat, painfully lost in the ever-present shadows of what I thought was God's silence. Have you experienced the same?

By now you may be questioning whether or not I'm truly an optimist at heart, but could it be that God actually speaks in ways we've never imagined—in ways that often defy human reason amid life's unanswered questions? Are we missing something? I think that in our efforts to understand God, we tend to unknowingly fashion him in our own image, because as I see it, there comes a point in life where human reason falls profoundly short. At this juncture we craft a mental caricature of God that we can understand and thus live with, and as a result, our lives and our faith often remain unchallenged and unchanged.

On the other hand, is it possible to come to terms with *faith* and *reason* in a way that moves us not simply out of the shadows of grief, loss, pain, and the heartbreak that comes with them, but to a place beyond our wildest dreams? Could it be that in our quest for answers to this apparent conundrum between faith and reason, there comes a *tipping point*, when in a moment in time, one's inability to reason or understand the action or inaction of God might actually strengthen one's faith, hope, and subsequent life? It's a perplexing and yet comforting mystery, which is curiously inescapable if we're willing to simply let God be God. I propose that this is the art of carefully navigating through the labyrinth of *limited reason* and *limitless faith*.

This intentionally short book is not an academic work, and while I note and share a handful of theological concepts, it's not a book of philosophy, psychology, or apologetics. What you're reading is just one man's story of a five-year journey through personal challenges and loss, and of how that journey cultivated the above-mentioned tension between faith and reason. Most books on faith and reason are intellectual endeavors, and while they most assuredly have their purpose and place, it's easy with them to get bogged down in details of the philosophical and logical arguments for the existence of this or that, or in the numerous apologetic proofs that build a case for the Christian faith—which often include a rational defense for evil, suffering, and loss. Real stories like yours and mine, however, add heart, soul, life, and meaning, and in the process they can also move us in the direction of pure hope, if we're willing to persevere as we navigate the rough waters of life. This is my desire for you and your journey of faith in a life that can be so very confusing and often wearisome.

Have you ever noticed when looking at railroad tracks that they seem to merge together off in the distance, but in reality they never do? It's an illusion. I submit that faith and reason are much the same, in that while they may lead us in the same general direction, they too rarely, if ever, merge—and furthermore, as I've mentioned, one of them will ultimately fall short. Essentially, this book attempts to deal with this phenomenon, but it's also a book with no tangible answers to our questions of why God does or doesn't do anything, for if we knew the answers, I suspect they wouldn't really help that much. They would simply lead us to more unanswerable questions. The raw beauty and majestic nature of hope isn't always found in the answers to our questions of "Why, God, why?" and "When, God, when?" Yes, hope is real, but it's often unreasonable. It's genuine, and yet sometimes evasive. It's heartfelt, and yet often mystifying. Oddly enough, however, hope has a name, and it is in this name that many place their unwavering trust. For some this is downright foolish, and yet for others it's a never-ending and often unexplainable way of life in a world that doesn't always make sense.

As always, I hope you enjoy my story.

Ron

A *fool* at heart...

Introduction

It was Monday, December 23, 2013, and as I sat there in the chair, drinking my morning coffee, I began to look around. It was then that I noticed the room was basically empty. I was in a corner of the rather large living room, facing the dining room, and the only items in both rooms were a small coffee table, a floor lamp, and the chair upon which I was sitting. As I sat there, it dawned on me: *what I see here is a metaphor for my life*. Before I arrived, the house had been full of furniture and life, but the family of five who'd lived there for fourteen years had moved on. When I arrived, it was just me and a few bits and pieces of what I needed for my stay as the interim pastor, my first assignment after retiring from church planting three months earlier. I was both thankful and thrilled at the opportunity to once again play a part in a local church. The church had some wonderful people, but this assignment would be so very different. This time I was alone. The four most important people in my life, the ones who had carried and supported me along the twenty-year journey of vocational ministry, were nowhere to be found. They were all gone, the last one being my younger brother, Mike, who had passed on Friday, July 27, 2013, at 6:45

a.m. No one had seen it coming. Three days later, on July 30, I did my little brother's funeral.

Without question, Mike was my lifelong best friend. We talked on the phone almost every day, and in a span of ten days, he'd gone from the diagnosis of liver cancer to breathing his last breath. Three weeks before his death, he and I went to a Detroit Tigers game, and we bantered back and forth about my retirement, which was set for September of 2013. He was going to retire in April of 2014, and along the way, we were marking plans; we talked regularly about enjoying the retired life to its fullest. We dreamt of traveling with our families to places unknown. He promised to regularly take me fishing on his boat, his pride and joy. We longed to hang out with each other like it was when we were kids, but we couldn't when our careers took us in different directions. As I looked around the house that morning, I wondered, how did I get here? What happened? It seemed like another shattered dream. Once again, God didn't make sense. Once again, it wasn't supposed to be this way. It wasn't fair. Mike, my precious younger brother, and I had plans!

In January 2014, my two best friends came over for a visit. They told me they were going to be in the area anyway, but I'm fairly certain they were simply checking in on me, as they had regularly done over the past three and a half years since my late wife's passing. I gave them a tour of the church, and we had lunch in the mostly empty house. I then took them to a nearby state park that has all the outdoor activities one could imagine: ice skating rinks, cross-country skiing, and snowshoe and hiking trails that go on for miles through the hills and along the shoreline of Lake Michigan. As a long-distance runner who has run many trails in Michigan's state parks, I had no doubt that this would be where I would spend most of my spare time wading through my thoughts about life and faith. But it was during our visit to the park that my late wife's best friend said to me, "You know that none of this would be possible if Bonnie was still here, or even if Mike were still alive. It's in your 'new life' that you now have an unwelcome freedom. I know you didn't want it, but you now have it." Her comment wasn't like the other comments that had come my way over the years. It was a thoughtful insight that came from her heart and soul at the right time and the right place, but at the time, I had no clue what she was trying to tell me. I was unaware of how my losses and accumulated grief were affecting my reasoning and my faith. She could see what I was unable to see and understand. For how my soul and the pain resting therein were clouding my faith and ability to reason was yet to be discovered in full. What I also failed to realize at the time was that my experiences and subsequent story of grief and loss were the same experiences and story shared by those who had walked with me every step of the way; my two best friends refused to let me drift into a life of acute loneliness.

Compounded grief and loss are so misunderstood, and there are no easy answers to how the complexity of it all affects our thoughts, our emotions, our actions, our relationships, and our faith. If we're unwilling to patiently walk through it all with some help from those few whom we trust we avoid the difficult questions, or worse yet, pursue quick solutions. Fact is, in our losses we will grieve forever, and how we move forward, and the decisions we make along the way, make all the difference. Notice I said "move forward" and not "move on," for "moving on" suggests we forget the past and simply move on to the next relationship, the next adventure, or the next whatever that offers us a distraction from what's truly going on deep inside our heart and soul. Little did I realize at the time that in some way, my interim role was doing just this, and it was my best friends who ultimately helped me see that my new life was yet to be discovered. Life is an ongoing contradiction of emotion, intellect, will, and heart. It's a mystifying confluence of what doesn't always make sense. How God fits into all of it and where he is when we truly need him are sometimes grand, unanswerable mysteries. Our existence on this earth is often a living, breathing paradox of real life, faith, and reason.

This book talks about my personal discovery of a new life in the middle of what can't be reasoned or explained, and if you have walked in similar shoes of loss, setbacks, and heartbreak, you are well aware that the vast majority of answers offered by people with good intentions are of no measurable comfort, and while they are most assuredly offered in love, they are not really all that helpful (e.g., "Ron, you need to *move on*."). In the deepest and darkest moments of our losses, we sometimes stop asking questions. It is these very struggles, as well as the friendships that carried me along the journey, that prompted this book. If you're someone who is patiently walking alongside someone like me, I want to encourage you to never stop. While at the time they may go unnoticed, your ongoing love and your very presence are pure and treasured gifts. For with people like you in our lives, it is possible to one day to arrive at a place where people like me can once again love completely without complete understanding.[1]

This is the third book of a trilogy that speaks to the conundrum of loss and discovery and the possibility of climbing out of the shadows of silence into the often-indescribable hope of a new life. In essence, what you are about to read centers on one thing: *foolish trust.* To get there, however, we need to explore a few things: Chapter One, "Unanswered Questions"; Chapter Two, "An Attempt at Reason"; Chapter Three, "Foolish Trust"; and the epilogue, "The Fellowship of Fools." My dream of dreams is that along the way, you too will discover that amid all the uncertainty, chaos, and theological confusion, there is something beyond reason waiting for you. Remember, hope has a name, and he knows you better than you know yourself. So press on, and as you slowly *move forward* in the fray of it all, let hope gradually emerge.

> *Where is the wise person? Where is the teacher of the law? Where is the philosopher of this age? Has not God made foolish the wisdom of the world? For since in the wisdom of God the world through its wisdom did not know him, God was pleased through the foolishness of what was preached to save those who believe.*[2]

CHAPTER I

Unanswered Questions

———

As the deer pants for streams of water, so my soul pants for you, my God.
My soul thirsts for God, for the living God.
When can I go and meet with God?
My tears have been my food day and night, while people say to me all day long,
"Where is your God?"
Why, my soul, are you downcast?
Why so disturbed within me?

—Sons of Korah[3]

Dyslexia: *any of various learning disorders associated with impairment of the ability to interpret spatial relationships or to integrate auditory and visual information, often resulting in difficulty learning to read.*[4]

Spiritual Dyslexia: *the impaired ability to process and comprehend spatial relationships, or first things first, as they relate to living what can best be described as a life of faith in God*

There are numerous Christ followers who regularly wrestle spiritual dyslexia, myself being among them. We tell stories of the inability at times to process and make theological sense of life and what's going on both in and around us. We often wonder why we get thrown messy curve balls that defy our understanding of it all. We tend to interpret life only through the grid of the here and now. We're not all that pleased with canned spiritual responses to life's setbacks and disappointments. We long for genuine answers and meaningful solutions. We're uncomfortable with not knowing why life unfolds the way it does and with the "silence" (or lack of response) in our prayer lives. Then, in a dyslectic sense, we get confused when God seems so very distant, and even though we keep this feeling to ourselves, we often construe him as uncaring. Am I the only one who wrestles with this, or at times do you feel the same?

On August 6, 1996, I was invited by a congregation to help replant their church in Ann Arbor, Michigan. It was my first church after graduation from Bible college and seminary, and if you're curious about the path that took me to biblical and theological study, as well as church planting, I've included a brief summary of events in the endnotes.[5] Nevertheless, by the time I arrived in Ann Arbor I was forty-eight and thrilled to be part of this new adventure. However, within a few months of my arrival I had my second encounter with a question that, as I see it now, has no satisfactory answers. Up until then, however, I was fairly confident in my ability to reason the movements of God. After all, I was a student of Bible theology, apologetics, and logic. On numerous occasions I would conduct classes that walked those who were curious through the various "arguments" for God's existence and the veracity of the Scriptures. I would present evidence supporting the divine claims of Jesus, his preexistence, his miraculous work, his life-giving sacrificial work on a cross between two thieves, and his bodily resurrection after said atoning death—all of which I still acknowledge as true and thus firmly embrace as an ongoing way of life. Yet within those few months after my arrival in Ann Arbor, I was invited to do the funeral for a young man tragically killed in a car accident, leaving his wife and his eight-year-old son behind. A few days before the funeral, the young boy's mom asked me to come over and chat with them. She had questions. This little boy who had just lost his dad had questions. It was then that I again realized I had no rational answers.

Two years earlier, in a series of job interviews, my inability to satisfactorily answer questions concerning why God "takes away" parents via tragic death had disqualified me from the pastor job for which I was interviewing. I was extremely disappointed, but not disheartened, so I had pressed on toward the next opportunity to pastor a church. For whatever reason, however, this little boy's questions now hit me profoundly hard, and not having any tangible answers for him made matters worse. As I look back, maybe it was then that a certain level of ambiguity between my faith and my ability to reason was birthed.

Spring forward to April of 2008. I was the church planter of a new church. After an article ran in the local newspaper about the church, whose motto was "compassion rules," a middle-aged man and his wife began showing up. Once we got to know each other, the man and I would meet somewhat regularly at a local restaurant to discuss theology and apologetics—again, two of my favorite topics. The conversations were candid, lively, and intellectually engaging. Our friendship was growing, and my wife and I were invited over for dinner on a handful of occasions. Over the ensuing months, however, what began to emerge during our conversations were uneasiness and consternation. Behind his smile, there was something going on deep inside his soul that was driving him to disbelieve and distrust the God he had heard about over the years. He began to ask questions that once again pushed me to the brink of reason, and any answer offered seemed to push him farther off the cliff. He asked why bad things happen to good people, why God is unfair, why tragedy strikes the young and innocent, and why God is indifferent to suffering in the world. As time went on, I eventually concluded that his emotions were clouding his ability to reason and nothing I could say would change his mind; nor would any rational answer presented comfort his soul. In other words, his soul and his intellect were at odds. In retrospect, I suppose it was because of some significant heartbreaking event in his life that he had essentially walked away from a faith he once held, and while he may not have seen it, like many others, he found himself angry with God. How does a person get to this point in his or her faith walk?

There are times in our lives when faith and reason seem to never merge, and worse yet, the distance between them often appears impassible. Stories like the ones above are universal, and during the years following the abovementioned interactions, the mystery between faith and reason would become a recurring feature of my life. Tragedy, disappointment, loss, and the unanswered questions that come with them often push us farther from the beliefs we once held close. All too often we begin walking away from our faith amid life's unbearable storms. On more than one occasion, I've found myself asking the very same questions of God himself.

In my second book, *Crazy Shepherd, Crazy Sheep,* I tell of a time when I was so angry with God that I actually began throwing rocks at him when my wife's hip suddenly and without reason dislocated while on a mission trip to Mexico.[6] Upon our return home, she underwent the fourth of her five hip surgeries. Over the course of our thirty-seven years of marriage, I found myself asking why God said no to our dreams of having five children, no to three adoption attempts, no to the possibility of having grandchildren, no to a long and healthy life for my wife, and no to the fulfillment of our dream of growing old together. When we were first married, she was energetic, spunky, sports minded, and outgoing, and then, when she suddenly became seriously ill six months into our new life, I often asked God why she had to have so much pain, so many surgeries, so many setbacks, and more time in the hospital than one could imagine. The answers to these questions never came. Here's the point: my story is not that uncommon. Significant heartbreak and the unanswered questions riding its coattails arise almost every day. It's the nature of life on this blue marble, and all too often we're left sitting in an empty hallway somewhere, face in our hands, asking where God is in all of this. Silence. It's deafening.

In fact, while it may not be all that comforting, a life of unanswered questions is far from a new phenomenon. For proof, one need look no farther than the people of the New Testament, people who were marvelously faithful to the newly arrived self-proclaimed Messiah, Jesus. When you read of the people who faithfully followed him, and the stunning differences that played out in their lives, you're left asking the same questions you would if you were walking in their sandals. For example, why was James, one of the sons of Zebedee, executed, and yet his brother John managed to live a long and successful life?[7] Both were supremely faithful followers of Jesus, and I wonder what questions raced through the hearts and minds of Zebedee and his wife at the death of their son James? Did they get any satisfactory answers or reasons for such heartbreak? In another account in the lives of Jesus's trusted followers, why was John the Baptizer, the one who baptized Jesus and the one who once pointed to him and proclaimed, "Look! The Lamb of God who takes away the sin of the world," beheaded by a Roman official?[8] Jesus was in the area and must have known of John's situation, and yet he did nothing. Why? I often wonder what John's parents were thinking when they heard about, or maybe even witnessed, their son being senselessly executed. Did they receive reasonable or comforting answers to their questions of why this meaningless tragedy took place?

Finally, another telling and profoundly mysterious episode is found in the life of a young man by the name of Stephen, who was fully devoted to the Messiah. His faith was bold and confident, his life on fire, and yet for simply preaching the good news of Jesus's arrival, death, and resurrection, the crowd stoned him to death. Then, not long after his stoning, the one who stood by and watched with approval, Saul, was called by God to preach the very same good news.[9] Why? This doesn't make any sense to me. How would you explain this unjust and heartbreaking loss to Stephen's mom and dad? Pardon my cynicism, but what specific and comforting reasons would you offer them? How would you answer their questions about why this tragic and confusing series of events took place?

As I sat there at the kitchen table, the young boy who had just lost his dad asked me, "Mr. Ron, why did God take my dad to heaven?" I remember looking over at his mom, and her eyes told me that she too needed an answer. I remember my reply as if it were yesterday: "I don't know why God does what he does, or even if he does it. Sometimes there are no helpful answers to the questions we have. But I can tell you this: your dad would want you to hug your mom, to love her as much as he loved your mom, to cry together, to remember and talk about how much your dad loved you. And to also know that God, the one who gave us Jesus, and blessed your dad with you, will walk with you both every step of the way." He simply sat there with a puzzled look on his face, and I walked out of the little boy's house feeling like I'd let him down. To this day, the answer to this little boy's question still evades me.

I'm often asked when my struggle between faith and reason came to a tipping point. As I've already mentioned, heartbreak and grief and their struggles are accumulative. They live with us forever, but at some point along the way, we often find ourselves at a low point. Like so many who have walked a similar path, I never saw that point coming, and when it did come, I did my best to conceal it.

In February of 2013, while at a church conference, I came to the realization that my time at the church I'd planted in 2007 was over. My teaching and leadership lives were on autopilot, and I was buried so deep in my grief that I simply couldn't do it anymore. As I continued to wade through the ever-present pain, I became convinced that I was not the leader who could take the church to the next level. Each and every Sunday, as I looked around at those in attendance, I saw faces that seemed to wish I would simply stop talking about my grief. My leadership decisions were all over the map. I lost focus and interest at meetings. Each week, as I prepared for the Sunday message, met with various teams to plan outreach events, and made calls to address individual needs, my mind and heart were often somewhere else. I found myself making less and less phone calls. I did my best to cast a vision of the future, but lacked the energy, zeal, and passion to carry it out. Although I did my best to hide it, Christmas and Easter services were extremely painful for me.

While those in leadership and those who called the church their home were so very kind, understanding, and patient, for me, everything seemed to be falling apart before my very eyes. So even though the thought that I needed to walk away from the dream once shared and pursued with my late wife was more than I could bear, I decided to retire, and yes, move on. This was when my struggle with faith and reason reached its zenith. And then, to make matters worse, my younger brother Mike suddenly passed, and without warning I was blindsided by the debilitating affects of accumulated grief. As you have read, there was much leading up to this moment, it was no doubt the lowest point in my life. On the surface I kept a smile on my face and displayed a sense of false enthusiasm, but deep inside my heart and soul, I couldn't wait to run away to places unknown.

As Oswald Chamber noted, "We come to our wit's end, showing that we don't have even the slightest amount of confidence in

Him or in His sovereign control of the world. To us He seems asleep, and we can see nothing but giant, breaking waves on the sea ahead of us."[10] We all have unbearable losses and unanswered questions, and as we move to the next chapter, you will discover once again that my efforts at reasoning direct answers seemed to always fall short.

CHAPTER 2

An Attempt at Reason

———

Human reason, like a slow-moving train,
Will only take you so far.
At the end of the day, when you look back through the rain,
It's really not that far at all.

—Ron (August 6, 2014)

In the middle of my interim pastor role, during the summer of 2014, an especially dear friend, Janet, and I attended a three-day church conference on evangelism. It covered the various methods by which Christians share the good news of Jesus wherever they live, work, or attend school. It was an incredibly large conference, with some of the biggest names on the topics of faith and reason scheduled to offer their expertise. There were approximately three thousand people in attendance, and the majority of them were twenty-something. As it turned out, I had read a good number of the books written by the guest speakers; they were among my favorite authors. The conference was extraordinary, one of the most laid back and informative I had attended in some time. The speakers were engaging, and their material was thought provoking. It was good to just sit back and reexamine the logical arguments and philosophical rationale for believing in God and giving your life to Jesus. As I've mentioned, early in my life with Jesus and as I entered into vocational ministry, the many topics and approaches surrounding the larger question of faith and reason were near and dear to my heart and mind. Suffice it to say, early on, apologetics and reasoning toward one's faith in the living God were some of my primary interests, and during the conference I experienced a sort of reawakening of the enthusiasm also expressed by the three thousand attendees, who couldn't wait to get out there and make use of their newfound insights and methods. It was a great three days.

As the conference was coming to a close, however, my twenty-some years of pastoral ministry and my personal challenges began to once again overwhelm my mind. In the inner recesses of my heart, a sense of uneasiness emerged, and I began to realize there was something missing. It is here that I need to remind you that this book is not an academic work. It's not a work of philosophy or logic. It's just a peek into my personal challenges and struggles with faith and reason. That being said, what I sensed missing at this three-day conference was *soul*. You know, that place deep inside the human heart where the sum of our emotions rests, the birthplace of every feeling you can imagine. What surfaced in my mind was the notion that this was precisely where the tension between faith and reason reaches its tipping point, that moment when our soul cries out for more answers, none of which seem satisfactory. I wanted to stand up and proclaim, "I'm a deeply wounded and heartbroken follower of Jesus. My wounds and heartbreak defy any endeavor at reasoning them away or rationalizing their existence." But I didn't, and as I sat there, somewhat at a loss, I began to wonder if there were others like me in the crowd. My experience, however, shows that I wasn't alone.

At this conference it occurred to me that this ever-present hollow place between faith and reason should not be ignored, nor glossed over with "reasonable" attempts at explaining away the tragedy, suffering, and heartbreak of this life. Often such attempts are what theologians and apologists call theodicies (i.e., theological arguments for why God allows evil and suffering in this world). As my friend and I drove home, I began to ask myself, could it be that tension itself is just part of the role that reason plays in our journey of faith? In other words, if reason is the quest for substantial answers, and faith is something expressed when said answers are nowhere to be found, then is it possible or even necessary to reconcile them? At the time I wasn't quite sure, but this I knew: amid our unwelcome and *unreasonable* wounds is the need at some level for a reasoned faith. For some of us, this is what creates the ongoing tension between faith and reason, and I suspect this is why far too many tragically walk away from a faith that was once held so firm.

Reasoning toward One's Faith

I believe it was St. Augustine who suggested that reason comes before faith and faith comes prior to a fuller understanding of said faith. To be sure, professing faith in God and his son, Jesus Christ, involves some level of reasoning. After all, as my brother has often reminded me, "Who in his right mind wants to believe in something that doesn't make any sense?" He raises a valid point. While reason may not be the starting point of everyone's faith journey, why on earth would anyone want to believe in something that can't be reasonably explained as authoritative and valid? In other words, one's faith in God has to possess some level of reason before one can be willing to give one's entire self to a life of following him. While how far people travel down the path of faith will most assuredly differ from person to person, this is precisely where faith and reason thrive, and where at some level, inquiry into theology and apologetics—intentional or not—plays an important role in one's journey toward a living and effectual faith. Fact is, it has been this way for some time.

For example, when you look back at the first disciples of Jesus, you'll see that each in his own way wanted some evidence, or proof, that Jesus was who he said he was: the Messiah who was promised by the prophets of old. Christ's travels with said disciples, therefore, are replete with actions that firmly support his claims to be the Messiah (e.g., healings, casting out demons, calming the sea, walking on water, forgiving sins, raising the dead, his death on the cross, and ultimately his own bodily resurrection). While it's not the purpose of this book to present the evidence for how these various actions took place and whether they can be trusted, suffice it to say that the early followers of Jesus wanted some reasonable proof that Jesus was indeed the much-anticipated Messiah. Therefore it makes sense that the same is true of us in our early following of Christ. Again, while how the process starts and how far one travels down the parallel tracks of faith and reason are different for everyone, examining the evidence and making a reasoned decision is part of the journey. Whether intentional or otherwise, this is the primary role of apologetics: reasoning toward one's faith.

One's World View

Whether we recognize it or not, we all have a world view that determines our perspective on most everything, including God, reality, knowledge, morality, and humankind. Our world view ultimately determines how we make decisions and move through our lives day to day. Additionally, our world view is significantly shaped, stressed, or challenged by our family background, and this is especially true with regard to how we are treated by our parents early in life. In many ways, our father is our first glimpse of God. Those who have had a loving parental father often have a less difficult time embracing God as their Father as those who have experienced the pain of parental abuse. Our successes, setbacks, and other major life events also play a formative role in the shaping of our world view, and often these experiences push us to the tipping point of either embracing or doubting various aspects of our world view, especially with regard to our faith in God. It has been said that when a person comes to faith in God, it often involves a significant shift in world view, and for some this shift is cataclysmic—a conversion from atheism to Christianity, for example.[11]

Another profound influence on our world view is the tension created when our soul cries out in pain and anguish to the point where a once-accepted and reasoned belief is pushed to its very limit, and this too can have cataclysmic effects. This is one of the primary reasons this book was written. With that being said, where does the soul fit in the grand scheme of who we are and how we navigate a life of faith?

The Four Parts of Us Humans

It's no secret that we humans are complex creatures made up of many parts, and it is the part called the soul where pain and anguish wreak havoc on our ability to reason. As you would expect, there are various theological and psychological views on what constitutes who we are and how we function, but for the sake of brevity and simplicity, let's keep our focus on our *intellect* (the mind), our *will* (action), our *heart* (the sum of who we are deep inside), and our *soul* (the seat of our emotions). I chose these four simply because of what Jesus told the young expert in the law when asked which of all the commandments is the most important: "The most important one…is this: 'Hear, O Israel: The Lord our God, the Lord is one. Love the Lord your God with all your heart and with all your soul and with all your mind and with all your strength.' The second is this: 'Love your neighbor as yourself.' There is no commandment greater than these."[12]

Whether we like it or not, each of the four parts affects the others. It can't be helped. For example, when we listen to music that deeply moves the soul, our minds may begin to hearken back to a time when we first fell in love, or a time when we lost someone very special. Likewise, fear is an emotion that can paralyze the will and stymie the intellect. Or, if you're like me, you can remember a time when you made a huge financial decision based purely on your emotions, when after all was said and done and you were driving home, you realized deep inside your heart that you had made a huge mistake.[13] It's the soul, the mind, the will, and the heart all working together. It's how we are wired. But what does this have to do with faith and reason? Everything.

We've already reviewed how we progress toward a reasoned faith through the mind, and it's not that difficult to figure out that when the mind is convinced, it is the will that moves us to do something about it (e.g., making a decision to follow Christ, or getting seriously involved with a charitable organization that serves the poor and homeless). Most assuredly, our emotions are also involved; we often describe this as our "heartstrings" being pulled. For example, we've all seen TV ads where humanitarian groups ask for funds to help the poor or house the homeless by using poignant images. I'm not taking shots at these much-needed campaigns to help others. However, as we've discussed, there are times when our emotions can get the best of us. So let's take a few moments and look at this mixture of intellect and emotion in terms of our faith, to see if it's possible for our emotions to lead us off course or leave us hanging in the hallway of uncertainty.

If a reasoned faith is based on certainty (truth), then what role do our emotions play? After all, each part of who we are works with and influences every other part. At some point for everyone, a reasoned faith eventually moves into the heart, which, like the conductor of an orchestra, begins to bring every other part into play. It's not as linear as it appears on paper, but rather as if it's all happening at the same time. Furthermore, our paths toward faith in God are remarkably diverse: some of us lean on our intellect long before the emotions come alive, while others feel faith long before the intellect becomes fully engaged. Either way, faith in God involves a confluence of mind and emotion and it is here where the heart often explodes with gratitude, passion, thrill, and wonder. It's a marvelous sight when it's all coming together. Yet as I have previously suggested, when the soul cries out in overpowering pain, it often trumps our intellect; for some of us, this is the moment in time when deep inside our heart, our faith begins to waver, or even to fall apart. Unfortunately, while they may indeed be heartfelt, our feelings are not always the best barometer of why something is or isn't taking place. When emotion trumps reason it significantly skews our perception of reality, which unfortunately, is not necessarily true—more on this later.

Theodicies: Why God Allows Evil and Suffering

When the wheels fall off the wagon of life, we want to know why. But this is also when people offer some of the most well-intended but untimely answers to the questions that surround our pain and loss. On more than one occasion, I was told that God wouldn't give me more than I could handle, that my late wife and my late brother were in a better place, that God had a purpose and a reason for what happened, that God needed them more than I did, that this was part of God's plan, that loss and suffering build character, and that death is just part of life on earth. Within a few months of my late wife's passing, with regard to my anguish, I was told to simply get over it. In all honesty, comments like these are not helpful at all, and on many occasions I just wanted to respond, "Shut up!" In retrospect, I suspect that people who make such comments are like me in that they too want answers. One of the most puzzling comments offered to me, however, was the idea that God wanted to use my heartbreaking losses to shape the fabric of who I am. This is called the soul-making theodicy, and at the time I found this explanation offensive and far from helpful.

Theodicies are attempts at reasoning the reality of evil and suffering in the world, and there are a handful from which to choose.[15] Admittedly, theodicies are important lines of reasoning as it relates to the philosophical and theological questions and challenges of the Christian faith. But while they may sound good in the classroom or the around the office water cooler, they never spoke to or even came close to helping mend the deep wounds of my soul. I could not find a way to reason away the pain. My soul's anguish trumped my ability to reason my way through plausible answers, and maybe, just maybe, it's the same for you.

The Principle of Limitation

Again, with a certain degree of regularity, we find ourselves grappling with the following: Why does God cause/allow/ignore

_____ (fill in the blank)? From here it's a short step to asking the next question: Why is God so distant and uncaring? Then, as it was for the friend I mentioned earlier, the end result is often a heart that says, "This is not the type of god I want to follow." What we read and what we see going on around us often don't align with our reasoned sense of justice and fairness, and we wrestle with this grand tension at every level of our being—with our senses, our emotions, our will, and our intellect. Unfortunately, as I have suggested, any and all attempts at reasoning will at some point fall desperately short, leaving us with nothing more than more questions to put on a list of answered questions.

Yet if one can demonstrate that within the whole of his or her being, there is an area of limitation—meaning an inability to do or become something—then is it also possible that there are limitations in other areas of our being? For example, consider the limitations of the human body: Can we morph ourselves from one life form to another? Or the limitations of the human mind: Can we imagine and then create anything out of nothing? Is it possible for the body to defy gravity on this earth without assistance? If the answer to one of these questions is no, then the possibility of other areas being limited is feasible. What about the limitation of human reasoning, or the inability to comprehend in full the actions, motives, and behaviors of God? Furthermore, is it possible that our reasoning abilities, or limitations thereof, skew or hinder our sense of justice and fairness? This is not my attempt at another iteration of a theodicy, but it is here, however, that I find myself concluding that human reasoning concerning the action or inaction of God has significant limitations.[16] Therefore, as I see it, it's not a stretch to suggest that it is exceedingly possible that reason, one rail of the railroad tracks, will at times fall profoundly short. But by no means is this realization new.

After giving one of the most in-depth and concise descriptions of the nature of the human condition and how God reconciles this condition, the apostle Paul, who I've quoted below, explodes into an extraordinary doxology. Here human reason is revealed as clearly having limitations regarding the action or inaction of God:

> Oh, the depth of the riches both of the wisdom and knowledge of God! How unsearchable are His judgments and unfathomable His ways! For who has known the mind of the Lord, or who became His counselor? Or who has first given to Him that it might be paid back to him again? For from Him and through Him and to Him are all things. To Him be the glory forever. Amen.[17]

If the magnitude of power behind Paul's words isn't enough, there is one word that stands out as it relates to our inability to reason away or understand in full God's action or inaction: *unfathomable*.

On one occasion Paul Jenkinson, a good friend and campus pastor of Oak Point Church of Milford, Michigan, mapped out the history and use of the word *unfathomable*. In short, the word dates back to the very early navigation methods of sailors, for whom it was especially needed as they approached the shoreline, when they would need to check the depth of the water with a higher degree of regularity. They did so by pounding on the inner hull of the ship. This pounding emitted a sound, at which point the sailors would measure the time it took for the sound to return. They would then shout out the water's depth in terms of fathoms. The longer the time between pounding on the ship's hull and the return sound, the deeper the water, but when the water was far too deep for the sound to return, the one making the measurements would cry out "Unfathomable!" In other words, the depth was immeasurable. Or as my friend Paul suggests, "We're in deep water." Suffice it to say, the same can be said of our efforts to fully comprehend God. When we try to reason God's motives and purposes, we too find ourselves in deep water; these things are unfathomable.

As I discovered at the church conference with Janet, our wounds wreak havoc in the depths of our souls and play a significant role in our faith, but unfortunately, they are all too often ignored. We conveniently repress them, for who wants to be known as someone who is deeply wounded? Woundedness brings with it a stigma of weakness, especially for men. As I mentioned earlier, I was told that I needed to "move on" more than once. But people who say this don't get it: there are some wounds from which you simply never move on. You just get up every day and try your best to take one step forward.

My experience with people like me, who have suffered the wounds of loss in any of its countless manifestations, tells me that for most of us, the soul trumps reason and the intellect. At the end of the day, all we have left is an insecure, wavering, and tentative faith. All too often it is the soul that pushes one's reasoned faith to its limits and beyond. This is where faith and reason part company. In other words, reasoning toward faith most definitely has its place, but in my story, there came a moment in time when the rail of reason abruptly ended, and I suspect it may be the same for you or someone you know. Human reason, like a slow-moving train, will only take you so far. At the end of the day, when you look back through the rain, it's really not that far at all. And herein rests the tipping point in one's life with God.

Lingering behind this tension lurk questions for which we now move to the next chapter. For when the soul takes over, and reason escapes us, what does it mean to believe? In other words, what is faith?

Chapter 3

Foolish Trust

———

Memo

Dear friends,

I can't thank you enough for your prayers and support over the past two weeks. My brother, Mike's, passing happened so very quickly; it caught all of us off guard, because six weeks ago he was fine. The raw emotions that I'm feeling are so very familiar; we've traveled this road before, haven't we?

For the longest time, I've known that when faith is pressed to the limit of reason, God does his best work; desperation is the secret place inside where one's faith is molded into a paradoxical mix of dependence and joy. It's a mystery, really, but one that need not make sense to be real and subsequently embraced in an almost marvelously defiant life of limited reason and limitless faith.

Ron

July 31, 2013

Spiritual truth is learned through the atmosphere that surrounds us, not through intellectual reasoning. It is God's Spirit that changes the atmosphere of our way of looking at things, and then things begin to be possible which before were impossible.

—Oswald Chambers, *My Utmost for His Highest*

F^{aith} is a funny word. It is universal, found in almost any arena of life. After all, faith can move mountains, right? Just keep the faith! You got to believe! Hang in there and hold on to your faith! *Faith* is also used as a comfort word, and rightfully so. But as it relates to one's life with God, what does *faith* actually mean?

Vine's Expository Dictionary of New Testament Words maps it out quite clearly, but the term's original meaning gets easily obscured in the everyday challenges and complexities of a busy life. The meaning of faith has taken on many shapes, sizes, expressions, and manifestations. Its application is as varied as those who use the word. Over time and various cultural trends, *faith* has become a catchall word that can mean almost anything.

In the context of life with God, however, the original and intended definition of *faith* is "trust, trustworthiness; a bringing together of belief and the contents, or object, of one's belief."[18] To have faith is to believe. To have faith is to trust. Thus to have faith, to believe, and to trust are three expressions of the same original thought. These words are for all intents and purposes interchangeable. Often the intended meaning of *faith*, however, leaves us feeling uncomfortable; a sense of uneasiness creeps in. Quite frankly, as it is lived out in a relationship with God, *faith* is far from a comfort word, especially when it's so very difficult to trust and believe when you're at the end of your rope, facing unexplainable losses or sitting in an empty hallway with your head in your hands. For some of us, trusting God when our ability to reason falls short is easier said than done. It's like jumping off a cliff with no parachute, no safety net, no bungee cord, and no idea of whether or not you'll even survive the fall.

On the other hand, faith is not the absence of doubt, nor an illusive endeavor that leads nowhere in particular. If you know the story of Thomas, one of the original disciples of Jesus, you are well aware that he had his fair share of doubts and yet was continually embraced by Jesus. Authentic faith is an invitation by Jesus to willingly merge trust and dependence on him. It transcends circumstance and situation, and yet at the same time, as with Thomas, it often leaves us with unanswered questions. It's something we experience at our very core and readily enter. It's a humble, ongoing walk or conversation with God that leads to a life of steadfast confidence and total reliance on him. It affects the sum total of who we are. Authentic faith, albeit unexplainable and unreasonable at times, is an ongoing convergence of mind, soul, will, and of course, heart. As expressed or lived out in its original meaning, faith affects how we both approach God and interact with one another. It affects how we treat our spouse and our children. In other words, faith affects the manner by which we deal with most everything that life throws our way. Fact is, you can't separate your faith from your life.

One of the most definitive descriptions of faith I've read is found in a book entitled *My Utmost for His Highest*. It is here that Oswald Chambers puts it all on the line: "[The only way to move about in our new life is to] have a simple, perfect trust in God— such a trust that we no longer want God's blessings, but only want God himself. Have we come to the point where God can withdraw the entirety of his blessing from us without our trust [faith] in him being affected?"[19]

As you can see, *faith* is far from a comfort word. Properly understood, faith is something that many of us struggle with or simply fail to internalize when pushed to certain limits. But more important than faith itself is the object of one's faith, and it is here that the following of Jesus is unique. In other words, the object of one's faith, belief, and trust is the crucial factor. As you are most likely aware, there are many objects of faith from which to choose, and hence it is essential that we choose wisely.

As we have discussed, one of the primary roles of apologetics is to help us reason our way to acknowledging Jesus as the only plausible option. This being so, I've listed some of the most trusted apologetic resources to help you in your journey of faith and reason (see End Note 11). Even then, however, when you do find your way to trusting Jesus with all that you are, there will be those who think that you're foolish. As they say, it "comes with the territory." Trusting Jesus is a reasoned faith, as I mentioned in Chapter Two, but what we're talking about now is the tipping point between faith and reason—when trusting doesn't stack up to what we're feeling in our souls or perceive as reasonable in our minds. And this leads us to perceptions, reality, and truth.

One of the few constants in our cosmos is change. With each passing second, the cosmos is slowly morphing into new shapes and sizes. It's always expanding and contracting. Over the millennia, stars, planets, and solar systems come and go. There is no stopping it. It's out of our control, an irrefutable fact of life. Now, if this is true of our universe, how much truer is it in the lives of those who inhabit the universe? In other words, if change is a constant in the "space" that surrounds us, it's also a constant in the "space" within us. Change, then, is also a fact of life, and it too comes in many shapes and sizes. It comes and it goes. Some changes we cause, and yet other changes arrive on the scene unannounced, by no fault of our own. Some changes are welcome, and yet others are far from it and often leave us wandering in a cloud of heartbreak and disappointment. Some changes are rather small, and others inexplicably life altering. The hard truth of the matter, whether we like it or not, is that change is unavoidable and affects almost every part of our world view.

Over the years I've had the privilege of interacting with those who wrestle with changes that come unexpectedly, changes that push them into the inner world of heartache, disappointment, mourning, loneliness, and sorrow: from divorce, job loss, failure, and chronic illness, to the loss of a spouse. One is neither greater nor lesser than the others. Regardless of how it manifests, heart-ache is heartache, grief is grief, disappointment is disappointment, and loss is loss. What I've noticed, however, is the need for answers, and when said answers are fleeting, it is often suggested that we search for some perspective on what God is doing to us amid it all. In other words, when "the wheels fall off the wagon," God must be "up to something." Or, putting it a bit more mildly, God can most certainly use our circumstances to our benefit. It's as if God is al-ways trying to mold us through the ups and downs of life. As I see it, on the surface this seems reasonable, but at the end of the day, it's just another attempt at an answer designed to help us muddle through life's setbacks. Quite honestly, most "answers" are not that comforting, and I find myself relying on someone else's ability to make sense of it all.

Trust in God, however, is birthed when everything else falls short—everything, including any attempt at reasonable explana-tions for why an event or change is taking place. Again, it is this level of trust that at times seems so very foolish, but it is here that a life of resolute faith in God truly begins—when he is all that we have left. These are without a doubt the most challenging and over-whelming times in the faith journey of a Christ follower. I guess this is why it is called foolish trust.

As I mentioned in Chapter Two, in many ways our father is our first glimpse of God, and thankfully, I'm one of the fortunate ones in that my father was one of the most gentle and even-tempered men I've ever known. Like most kids, I liked ice cream, but when the ice-cream truck visited our neighborhood, I was always left out due to a significant lack of funds. So in order to have enough cash for ice cream, at the age of about six, I began stealing pennies from my dad's dresser. This went on for a short time, but of course he discovered my thievery and promptly called me into the living room, where he asked me to sit on his lap. He then looked at me and said, "Ronnie, why didn't you ask me for help? Why didn't you come to me when you needed a few cents? I may not have given you the money, but I would have told you how to get it without stealing. Son, I love you, and always will. Please don't steal from me again." That was it. That's all he said, and it was the end of it. At such a young age, I had no clue about deep spiritual issues, but this was my first glimpse of God the Father, regardless of whether my dad handled it this way for this reason. This experience may have set a foundation I would need much later in life, at a time when I was surrounded by the unwelcome life changes mentioned earlier and needed to simply trust my Father.

Now, as I sit back and scan the landscape of my own life, I see a different person than I was five years ago. Just like for many of you, changes emerged for me during times of significant loss, both unexpected and uninvited. Nonetheless, such life-altering changes leave us with decisions to make. How will we navigate these changes? How will our choices affect our family and friends? Most assuredly, how we wade through these questions is very important, but the much larger question at hand is this: During times of crisis, will our choices affect our faith, or will our faith affect our choices?

On the surface, the answer to this question seems simple enough, but when reason falls short, which will it be? These are the tipping points in life, and at each one we must choose. I'm not suggesting that this is easy—far from it. What I am suggesting is that there are times in life when we should simply let God be himself and trust him when reason evades us. Again, to some this is Pollyanna-like foolishness, and yet to others who have walked in our shoes, foolish trust is a way of life. Again, trust is only trust when we're left with no answers to the gut-wrenching theological questions that often race through our hearts and souls. Fact is, if we had the answers, we wouldn't need faith. Some call this *fideism*: burying your head in the theological and philosophical sand, not facing the facts that others perceive as true. But as I wrote in *Crazy Shepherd, Crazy Sheep*, the most challenging layer of life is the layer of our perception. For example, last year I was having a cup of coffee with a friend when he told me that he was outside the scope of God's love. His actions over time had led him to believe that God no longer loved him, cared about him, or even knew he existed. This was his perception, his reality. So there he sat, head in hand.

What we perceive to be real is not always so, however, and sometimes we need to step back, wait, and let God intercede and peel the layers of perception away. In my friend's case, he perceived that God didn't love him, and so during his time of deep crisis, with some help from a trusted friend, he began to step back and look closer at the many ways in which God had already demonstrated his divine love to him. He began to slowly climb out of the darkness of God's silence and into the light of pure hope. At first, trusting God in the lowest point of his life, a time when reason escaped him, seemed unfounded. His perceptions were leading him down the wrong track, to nowhere in particular. Then one day he discovered that he was in good company—the company of fellow fools, of those who choose to let their unreasoned trust in God affect their choices when the bottom falls out beneath them.

I wish I could tell you when my wrestling match between my faith and reason came full circle. But it's more of an ongoing process than an event. In many ways, foolish trust is the art of *marvelous defiance*, an ongoing and never-ending engagement of our will in the midst life's uncertainties. Quite unexpectedly, however, it leads to the path of true freedom in the face of suffering, heartbreak, and life's reason-defying challenges. Is there anyone who can truly comprehend the tension between God's love and human suffering, or God's power and the existence of hideous diseases that take the lives of those we hold so dear? Marvelous defiance, a willing juxtaposition of faith and life, kicks in when reason runs short; it's a life-altering determination to relentlessly seek God amid silence, peace amid turmoil, and a modicum of stability even when life is falling apart before your very eyes.

This is why faith and trust are two sides of one coin; you can't have one without the other. By no stretch of the imagination is faith easy; it's a necessary and ongoing struggle between theology and life that in due course shapes the very essence of our inner lives. Yet this concept is so very misunderstood in many expressions of today's Christianity. After all, would complete understanding really solve anything? Would knowing why make us feel any better about what's happening around us? For me, foolish trust is an enigma really, but one that need not make sense to be real and subsequently embraced in an almost marvelously defiant life of limited reason and limitless faith.

Unwavering trust in God is both foolish and wise at the same time, and if this isn't enough, like my friend mentioned above, you'll soon discover that you're actually in good company—a rather large fellowship of sorts.

Epilogue

A Fellowship of Fools

There are only two constants in life, the heartbreaking sting and agony
of death, and the breathtaking love and grace of God.
One steals the life of those you cherish. . .
The other reminds you that he cherishes you.
One drags us down. . .
The other lifts us up.
One is liar and a thief. . .
The other is so very faithful and true.
One pierces our heart and soul. . .
The other tenderly pieces it back together again.
One turns our world upside down. . .
The other ever so gently turns it right-side up.
One pushes us to the brink of anger and disappointment. . .
The other whispers in our ear, "That's okay. I'm still here,
walking with you, side by side."
One rips the life out of us. . .
The other breathes it back in again.

One pushes us off the cliff of reason, grief, and loneliness...
The other reaches down deep inside and whispers,
"I will never leave you nor forsake you. I will always be with you. I am the
Author of life, joy, and peace. You have nothing to fear."

—Ron Gelaude, July 31, 2013, at Mike's funeral

Once again, thanks for reading my story. As I mentioned in the introduction, this is not a book with any tangible answers to why God does or doesn't do anything. It's simply an invitation to a way of life among those who have walked in our shoes. We need those who faithfully walk with us every day. In an odd way, to know there are people like you, who wrestle with the same questions that fly around my head, gives me a measure of peace and comfort. Neither you nor I are alone in our struggles. We know there are no easy answers to life's most perplexing questions. Foolish trust is not the absence of continued, genuine inquiry and the growth that comes with it. Essentially, foolish trust revolves around and leads us to only one person, the author and perfecter of the hope we profess: Jesus Christ. He is the hope that is fixed and secure in every way. He is the only stable and certain aspect of our lives in an unpredictable and often confusing world. Yes, it seems foolish to some, but to the fellowship of fools, there is no better way to live and to love. He is the hope that transcends our need for answers, through whom we can discover authentic peace within our souls, the seat of our emotions. It is upon him, the foundation of life, that we can ultimately rest. The writer of Hebrews puts it this way:

God, wishing to show beyond doubt that his plan was un-
changeable, confirmed it with an oath. So that by two utterly
immutable things, the word of God and the oath of God, who
cannot lie, we who are refugees from this dying world might
have a source of strength, and might grasp the hope that he
holds out to us. This hope we hold as the utterly reliable an-
chor for our souls, fixed in the very certainty of God himself in
Heaven, where Jesus has already entered on our behalf.[20]

We must always keep in mind that how foolish trust works out
in our lives is as varied as those who embrace it. The idea behind
it all is not finding your way to more blessings from God or to so-
called solutions to our feelings. For a long time I struggled with the
reality that I would never be able to love again nor enter a life of
allowing someone else to love me. Over the years following my late
wife's passing, there were those who asked if I would ever marry
again. Their questions were genuine and well intended, but the mere
thought of it literally made me sick to my stomach. I would quickly
and without reservation reply, "Why on earth would I ever want
to go through what I'm going through again? My theological questions have never been answered, nor do I expect they ever will be.
My heartache is something I will never repeat. It's not worth it.
Please don't ask me this again." This was my perceived reality, and in
my heart, soul, and mind, it would remain this way for time eternal.
So I buried myself in teaching, writing in my journal every day, and
trail running to escape the struggles and the pain, and along the

way I actually wrote a few books about my story. It was this way for a long time.

In the conundrum of faith and reason, however, with time and (foolish) trust in God, the one who transcends both faith and reason, our heart and soul begins to heal in ways that we never see coming. As it turned out, my then-present reality was only one season among the many that came my way. The hopelessness I was feeling deep inside my soul at the time was most assuredly real, but the truth was that it wasn't for time eternal. This is what I could not see at the time. Suffice it to say, over time I've changed, and the thought of possibly living once and being loved twice is now a promise come true. Over the past four years, I've learned that truly loving someone and thus being loved in return is worth all the heartache that often comes with it. I think we never really know the depth of true love until we experience the depth of pain in our losses. This seems like an absurd comment, but it's the inescapable nature and essence of a life well lived on this earth. After all, it is God's Spirit that changes our way of looking at things, and then things begin to be possible that before were impossible.[21] Why am I unreasonably certain of this? Because the one upon whom this fool places his unwavering trust amid his answered questions is the one who made the following promise:

> Trust in the Lord and do good; dwell in the land and enjoy safe pasture. Take delight in the Lord, and he will give you the desires of your heart. Commit your way to the Lord; trust in

him and he will do this: He will make your righteous reward shine like the dawn, your vindication like the noonday sun.[22]

Maybe you've walked away from a faith once held in God, or maybe you're struggling with what's going in your life without answers. If so, once again I want to encourage you to never give up, to never stop asking questions. Moreover, never stop talking with your trusted friends who faithfully walk with you in your struggles, with those who refuse to let you remain lost in the valley of loss and failure. Let those who truly love you do so, for it's easy to seclude ourselves in loneliness and pain. Never stop seeking answers from God. While you may never receive an answer, he can handle your questions without judgment, and *he will never leave your side.*

Finally, if there is an answer offered in this book, maybe it's this: along the path of life, you will come across people just like you, those who need a warm smile and a friendly face from someone who has walked or is walking the same uncertain and often wearisome path. In other words, once again, people just like us need people just like you.

As the writing of this book unfolded, this has been my genuine hope and sincere prayer for you: that you find your way to a new or rejuvenated steadfastness of faith in the one and only Jesus Christ, and a renewed sense of pure hope in the life he offers without the answers we assume we need. Like it has been for me, may you too realize a reason-defying fullness of peace with God, a soothing of your soul deep within that only he can provide. And in closing,

I pray that you find it in your mind, heart, soul, and will to join the ever-growing fellowship of fools. Believe me: nothing would give me greater pleasure.

This is my story. It's now up to you to "write" your own. If I can do it, so can you.

—Ron Gelaude, one "fool" among many, 2015

About the Author

Ronald Gelaude is a former church-planting pastor with the Great Lakes Conference (GLC) of the Evangelical Covenant Church. Though he is retired, he continues to pursue God's call to (interim) pastoral service in various GLC churches and through his writing.

Gelaude holds a bachelor of religious education degree in pastoral studies from William Tyndale College, a master of theological studies degree from Michigan Theological Seminary, and a master of communication studies degree from Eastern Michigan University.

Combining his genuine desire to help others with his well-honed storytelling skills and unique life experiences, Gelaude has thus far authored three works of nonfiction, *The Religion of Jesus*, *Crazy Shepherd, Crazy Sheep*, and most recently, *Foolish Trust*, each of which chronicles major turning points in his spiritual journey and explains his compelling point of view as a follower of Christ.

End Notes

[1]   Adapted from the movie *A River Runs through It*. A Columbia Pictures film (1992).

[2]   I Corinthians 1:20–21

[3]   Excerpt from Psalm 42. Words that rang out during my most challenging times.

[4]   *The Free Online Dictionary by Fairfax.*

[5]   For the longest time I thought the message of Jesus was simply about life after death; what my post-life would encompass after all was said and done. At least this was the message wafting around in my head. The instinctive and irresistible draw to an off-road life of adventure, thrill, and exploration, at least in my view, was not compatible with the life that Jesus offered. After all, he and those who followed him were simply concerned about my ultimate destination, which I supposed was a good thing, if that's all there was to it. However, for a young boy who would someday hopefully become a young man, the life that Jesus offered seemed boring, mundane, and irrelevant. Then one day, many years later, I was introduced to Tom. At first glance he was just another seemingly bored out of his skull pastor who was going through the motions. I ultimately discovered, however, that Tom was very different than

any Christ follower I had ever met, and over time, we became good friends. Ever so slowly it was Tom who introduced me to the Jesus I had never met before, and before long I began to see what life could be like when viewed through a fundamentally different lens; the lens of a humble selfless servant, Jesus. In the coming years, after meeting Tom, I began to sense the nudge from God to become a pastor. I then entered into academic studies at a Bible College and Seminary. This is where my off road journey truly began as a church planter, someone who starts new churches (taken in part from *Crazy Shepherd, Crazy Sheep.* pages 4-5).

6   Ron Gelaude, *Crazy Shepherd, Crazy Sheep.* Copyright Ron Gelaude, 2013. All rights reserved. Page 52. Available at createspace. com/4503418.

7   Acts 12:1–3.

8   John 1:29.

9   Acts Chapters 8–90.

10   Oswald Chambers, *My Utmost for His Highest*, ed. James Reimann (Grand Rapids: Discovery House, 1992). Used by permission of Discovery House Publishers, August 12.

11   It is here that I need to once again remind you that this is not a work of philosophy and apologetics, and as such, the topic of world view is intentionally brief. If this discussion interests you, I highly suggest that you take some time and read *Faith and Reason*, by Ronald H. Nash. Other helpful books on faith and reason are *The Reason for God*, by Timothy Keller, *The Case for Faith*, by Lee Strobel,

and *The Reason Why*, by Mark Mittelberg. (My personal favorite is *The Reason for God*.)

[12]   Mark 12:29–31.

[13]   Another personal example of this is when I bought a very expensive boat because I "loved" it. It was an emotional decision. By the way, the saying that the best two days of a boater's life are the day he buys the boat and the day he sells it is true!

[14]   For example, 1) we suffer because of original sin, 2) pain and suffering are punishment for our sin, 3) it's a necessary dynamic and outcome of free will, 4) to have good, you must have evil, 5) the principle of sufficient reason (i.e., since God is all good, he must have a good reason for allowing evil, pain, and suffering), and 5) as mentioned above, the soul-making theodicy, just to name a few.

[15]   I suggest that limited reason is not a theodicy, because by the very nature of reason being limited, it's not a rational defense for evil and suffering. I'm no philosopher, but to me it's circular reasoning (i.e., "I reason that reason is limited").

[16]   Romans 11:33–36 (NASB)

[17]   Vine et al., *Vine's Expository Dictionary of New Testament Words*. Used by permission. Pages 222–223.

[18]   Oswald Chambers, *My Utmost for His Highest*, ed. James Reimann (Grand Rapids: Discovery House, 1992). Used by permission of Discovery House Publishers, October 23.

[19]   Hebrews 6:19–20. J. B. Phillips New Testament. Used by permission.

20   Oswald Chambers, *My Utmost for His Highest*, ed. James Reimann (Grand Rapids: Discovery House, 1992). Used by permission of Discovery House Publishers, October 12.

21   Psalm 37:3–6

20929315R00046

Made in the USA
San Bernardino, CA
29 April 2015